Kaplan Business Books

Finance Act 2022

The impact on your exams

ACCA – Taxation (TX – UK)

KAPLAN
PUBLISHING

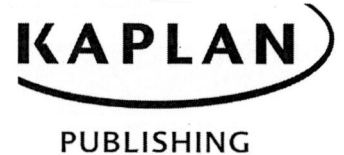

© Kaplan Financial Limited, 2022

All rights reserved. No part of this publication may be reproduced, stored in a retrieval system, or transmitted, in any form or by any means, electronic, mechanical, photocopying, recording or otherwise, without the prior written permission of Kaplan Publishing.

The text in this material and any others made available by any Kaplan Group company does not amount to advice on a particular matter and should not be taken as such. No reliance should be placed on the content as the basis for any investment or other decision or in connection with any advice given to third parties. Please consult your appropriate professional adviser as necessary. Kaplan Publishing Limited and all other Kaplan group companies expressly disclaim all liability to any person in respect of any losses or other claims, whether direct, indirect, incidental, consequential or otherwise arising in relation to the use of such materials.

FINANCE ACT 2022 – THE IMPACT ON YOUR EXAM

PREFACE

This booklet aims to provide a student-friendly summary of the key changes to UK tax rules introduced in the Finance Act 2022 (and associated changes made by other legislation).

It is a bespoke Finance Act summary, setting out the changes specifically for examination purposes.

It only includes changes with an impact on the ACCA Taxation (TX-UK) examination syllabus for the June 2023 to March 2024 sittings.

Most temporary tax changes made during the COVID-19 pandemic, such as the extension of some tax payment deadlines, and changes to certain VAT rates, have been excluded by the ACCA from the syllabus. Those rule changes are therefore not in this booklet. Students should use only normal tax rules, within the syllabus, for answers to the June 2023 to 31 March 2024 examinations. This booklet provides an easy way for students with prior knowledge of the TX syllabus before FA2022 to update their knowledge with the latest relevant tax changes.

It is an ideal way for students to refresh their knowledge on the key areas of change, without having to purchase and read a completely new Study Text (which will incorporate the changes but does not highlight where the changes are from previous studies).

This booklet also provides worked examples to illustrate the impact of the new provisions on examination-type questions.

This booklet is primarily aimed to help:

- those students retaking the TX examination

- those who started studying under the previous Finance Act but have deferred their first exam attempt to June 2023 or later, and

- those who have been successful at TX and are about to study for the ATX examination under the new Finance Act. For these students, retention of up to date knowledge of TX topics is an essential prerequisite to being successful at ATX. Many ATX tuition courses treat TX topic areas as assumed knowledge.

This booklet is therefore either essential reading (for the first two groups) or recommended reading (for the third group) before beginning a study course for the ATX examination sitting the exam in June 2023 onwards.

FINANCE ACT 2022 – THE IMPACT ON YOUR EXAM

CONTENTS

		Page
Introduction		5

Summary of update changes:

A	Syllabus and examination format changes	6
B	Finance Act 2022	10
C	Tax rates and allowances	23

Appendices:

1	Pro forma capital allowances computation – unincorporated businesses	29
2	Approach to capital allowances computational questions	31
3	Capital allowance illustrations	33
4	Time limits for elections and claims	36

NOTES

If you require a Study Text incorporating these changes, the FA2022 version of Kaplan Publishing's TX learning materials is available. This has been produced primarily for use by students sitting the examination in the year April 2023 to March 2024 for the first time. Please go to www.kaplanpublishing.co.uk .

The chapter references given at the head of each section in Part B of this booklet enable easy cross reference to the relevant chapter of the FA2022 version of Kaplan TX Study Text, but you do not need to have a copy of this version to benefit from this booklet.

KAPLAN PUBLISHING

FINANCE ACT 2022 – THE IMPACT ON YOUR EXAM

INTRODUCTION

The format of the ACCA TX computer-based examinations sat in June 2023 to March 2024 will be unchanged. The examination format is summarised in Section A of this booklet.

There have been some changes to the content of the TX syllabus, which are mainly due to the inclusions and exclusions of topics introduced in the Finance Act 2022. These are summarised in Section A; detailed information and examples of new areas are provided in Section B.

The ACCA have released information about the tax rates and allowances that will be provided in the June 2023 to March 2024 examination sittings. A full set of the tax rates and allowances, as they should appear in the examination is given in Section C.

TX-UK: TAXATION (FA2022)

A SYLLABUS AND EXAMINATION FORMAT CHANGES

1 INTRODUCTION

This section highlights the key changes in the syllabus and examination format that affect TX-UK for the June 2023 to March 2024 sittings of the TX-UK examination

2 NEW TOPICS INCLUDED IN THE SYLLABUS

The major topics which have been added to the syllabus following FA2022 are:

- Increase to the rate of income tax for dividend income (section 3.2.1)
- Changes to thresholds and rates for national insurance contributions (section 6.2)

3 TOPICS EXCLUDED FROM THE SYLLABUS

This is a list of changes made by FA2022, or by other legislation taking effect in the tax year 2022/23, which the ACCA have confirmed are not in the TX syllabus for the exams in June 2023 to March 2024:

- Future increase in corporation tax rate from April 2023
- Abolition of cross-border group relief for non-UK losses of EEA subsidiaries
- Minor changes to Real Estate Investment Trust rules
- Implementation of VAT rules in free zones
- VAT exemption for dental prosthesis imports
- VAT relief for energy saving materials
- New points system for late VAT returns
- Late payment and late submission penalties and interest harmonisation
- Reducing inheritance tax reporting requirements

4 EXAMINATION FORMAT

We are not aware of any proposed changes to the format of the examination at the June 2023 to March 2024 sittings but it is wise to check the ACCA Global website periodically for the exam information which is provided there.

Late changes announced by ACCA for any reason will be notified on MyKaplan wherever practicable.

The TX examination is in the following format:

The examination is in **THREE sections**, and is predominantly computational.

All questions are compulsory.

	Number of marks
Section A:	
15 objective test questions worth 2 marks each (Note 1)	30
Section B:	
3 objective test case questions worth 10 marks each (Notes 1 and 2)	30
Section C: (Note 3)	
One 10 mark constructed response (long) question	10
Two 15 mark constructed response (long) questions	30
Total	100

Notes:

1. Section A and B questions can be drawn from any area of the syllabus.

   Section A will be **15 objective test questions**, each worth 2 marks.

2. Section B will consist of **three objective test case questions**.

   Each question is a case study style question containing one set of information and five objective test questions worth 2 marks each. The objective test questions are based on the common scenario given. Each objective test case question is worth 10 marks in total.

3. Section C will consist of **three constructed response questions**; one worth 10 marks and two worth 15 marks.

   The 10 mark question can be drawn from any area of the syllabus.

   The two 15 mark questions will focus on two specific areas:

   – one focusing on income tax

   – one focusing on corporation tax.

   However, each of these questions could include a small number of marks in respect of other taxes.

   There is no set order for the Section C questions. In the specimen examination the 10 mark question appeared before the 15 mark questions, but the ACCA could change the order.

4. Any of the questions might include the consideration of issues relating to the minimisation or deferral of tax liabilities.

PASS MARK

The pass mark for all ACCA Qualification examinations remains at 50%.

DURATION OF EXAM

The syllabus is assessed by a 3 hour computer-based examination (CBE). Students will have up to 10 minutes to familiarise themselves with the CBE system before starting the exam.

Reading and planning remain crucial elements of your examination technique and it is important that you allocate time in the examination to this.

5 METHOD OF EXAMINATION: COMPUTER BASED EXAMINATIONS (CBEs)

All TX-UK examinations for the June 2023 to March 2024 sittings will be computer based.

OT questions in sections A and B of the CBE will be of **varying styles**. The types of objective test questions you could see in your CBE are as follows

Question type	Description
Multiple choice	Select one correct answer from a choice of four
Multiple choice – multiple correct answers	Select a given number of correct answers
Pull down list	Select one correct answer from a drop down list
Fill in blank	Input a numerical answer
Hot area	Select one or more areas in an image as a correct answer (e.g. true or false)
Drag and drop	Drag chosen answer(s) to other areas of the screen

Examples of questions in the different styles, as far as suited to TX, can be found in the Kaplan FA2022 Exam Kit.

5.1 Examination tips for CBEs

- On the ACCA website there is a CBE demonstration.

    It is ESSENTIAL that you attempt this before your real CBE.

    You will become familiar with how to move around the CBE screens and the way that questions are formatted, increasing your confidence and speed in the actual examination.

- Be sure you understand how to use the software before you start the examination.

- If in doubt, ask the assessment centre staff to explain it to you.

- Questions are displayed on the screen and answers are entered using keyboard and mouse.

- In addition to multiple choice type questions, CBEs will also contain other types of questions – see the table above.

    You need to be sure you know how to answer questions of all these types before you sit the examination, through practice.

TX–UK: TAXATION (FA2022)

B FINANCE ACT 2022

1 INTRODUCTION

This document highlights the key changes that affect the TX examination for the June 2023 to March 2024 sittings, caused by Finance Act 2022 or other legislation having effect in tax year 2022/23 and Financial Year 2022.

2 TAX RATES AND ALLOWANCES

Tax rates and allowances can change each tax year. A copy of the tax rates and allowances for FA2022, as expected to be provided in the TX CBE, is reproduced in Section C of this booklet.

The rest of Section B covers the effects of the rate changes and other legislative changes in FA2022.

It is broken down into the key tax areas as follows:

Section 3	Personal income tax
Section 4	Business income tax (no changes)
Section 5	Pensions (no changes)
Section 6	National insurance contributions
Section 7	Capital gains tax
Section 8	Inheritance tax (no changes)
Section 9	Corporation tax (no changes)
Section 10	Value added tax
Section 11	Tax administration

3 PERSONAL INCOME TAX

3.1 Key changes

Key changes to personal income tax are covered as follows:

- income tax band limits and rates (section 3.2)

- income tax personal allowance (section 3.3)

- fixed amount of personal allowance transferable to spouse or civil partner (section 3.4)

- employment benefit rules (section 3.5)

- the basic rate restriction re residential property income finance costs has been removed from the tax rates and allowances (see section C)

3.2 Changes in income tax band limits and rates (Chapters 2 and 3)

3.2.1 Income tax rate increase for dividend income for 2022/23

In 2022/23 the income tax rates for non-savings and savings income are unchanged from 2021/22. So in summary:

- the basic rate of income tax continues to be 20%
- the basic rate band limit remains at £37,700
- the higher rate of income tax continues to be 40%
- the additional rate of tax continues to be 45%, and continues to apply where taxable income exceeds £150,000.

When computing the income tax liability, personal pension contributions and gift aid payments extend the basic and the higher rate bands, by the amount of gross contributions and gross donations (after adding back all basic rate tax relief).

Illustration 1

Juanita has taxable income for the tax year 2022/23 of £160,000 which consists of £130,000 employment income and £30,000 property income. She makes personal pension contributions of £3,200 (net).

Juanita's income tax liability for the tax year 2022/23 is calculated as follows:

Juanita
Income tax computation – 2022/23

	Total	Non-savings income		
	£	£		£
Taxable income (Note)	160,000	160,000		
Income tax:		£		£
Non-savings income (W)		41,700	× 20%	8,340
		112,300	× 40%	44,920
	(W)	154,000		
Non-savings income		6,000	× 45%	2,700
		160,000		
Income tax liability				55,960

Working: Extended band limits

	BR Band	HR Band
	£	£
Current band limit	37,700	150,000
Add: Gross PPCs (£3,200 × 100/80)	4,000	4,000
Revised band limit	41,700	154,000

Note: Juanita has a PA of nil as her ANI > £125,140 – for reduction of PA, see 3.3.2

The income tax rates applying to dividend income in 2022/23 have been increased:

- falling in the basic rate band = 8.75%
- falling in the higher rate band = 33.75%
- falling in the additional rate band = 39.35%.

The order of taxing income remains unchanged, being as follows:

- first 'non-savings income' (e.g. employment income, trading income, property income)
- then savings income
- then dividend income.

Note that the increases to the tax rates applicable to dividends mean that incorporating a sole trader's business or partnership will no longer necessarily result in a tax saving.

The increased rates will also affect the decision as to whether to extract corporate profits as a dividend or as director's remuneration.

3.3 Changes to income tax allowances (Chapter 2)

3.3.1 No change in the personal allowance

The personal allowance to use in the examination for the tax year 2022/23 is £12,570.

3.3.2 No change to income limit for reduction of the personal allowance

The personal allowance (PA) continues to be reduced for an individual with income in excess of £100,000. This is referred to in TX rates and allowances as the 'income limit'.

Where a taxpayer's adjusted net income (ANI) exceeds £100,000, the PA is reduced by:

50% × (ANI – £100,000)

If necessary the reduced PA is rounded up to the nearest pound.

The ANI is calculated as follows:

	£
Net income	X
Less: Gross gift aid donations	(X)
Less: Gross personal pension contributions	(X)
Adjusted net income (ANI)	X

A taxpayer with ANI in excess of £125,140 in 2022/23 will therefore be entitled to no PA, as the excess income above £100,000 is more than twice the starting PA.

This figure of £125,140, above which you do not need to do a detailed PA adjustment working, is given in the exam tax rates and allowances for 2022/23.

Remember that if there are gift aid donations and/or personal pension contributions (PPCs), their gross amounts reduce the ANI figure and also extend the basic rate and higher rate bands when applying the correct rates of income tax to taxable income.

FINANCE ACT 2022 – THE IMPACT ON YOUR EXAM

Method

- Calculate the individual's net income and ANI for tax year 2022/23
- Adjust PA if ANI exceeds £100,000 – down to a minimum PA of £Nil
- Net income minus the available PA (as reduced) = taxable income
- Calculate income tax on taxable income, remembering that the basic rate band normal limit (still set at £37,700) and higher rate band normal limit (still set at £150,000) are extended for each individual, by gross gift aid donations and personal pension contributions.

Illustration 2

Jimi received dividend income of £117,000 during the tax year 2022/23. He paid a personal pension contribution of £9,500. These amounts are stated gross.

Jimi's income tax liability is calculated as follows:

Jimi
Income tax computation – 2022/23

	£
Dividend income	117,000
Less: Adjusted PA (W1)	(8,820)
Taxable income (all 'dividend income')	108,180

Income tax:

£		
2,000	× 0%	0
45,200	(W2) × 8.75%	3,955
60,980	× 33.75%	20,581
108,180		

Income tax liability	24,536

Workings

(W1) Adjusted PA

	£	£
PA		12,570
Net income (see note)	117,000	
Less: Gross PPC	(9,500)	
Adjusted net income	107,500	
Less: Income limit	(100,000)	
	7,500	
Reduction of PA (£7,500 × 50%)		(3,750)
Adjusted PA		8,820

Note: In this example, as there are no other sources of income and no reliefs, dividend income = total income = net income.

KAPLAN PUBLISHING

> (W2) **Extended band limits**
>
> | | BR Band £ | HR Band £ |
> |---|---|---|
> | Current limit | 37,700 | 150,000 |
> | Add: Gross PPC | 9,500 | 9,500 |
> | Revised limit | 47,200 | 159,500 |
>
> Jimi's taxable income exceeds the revised BR band limit, but is below the revised HR band limit (£159,500) where the additional rate would begin to apply if taxable income of 2022/23 were higher.

3.4 Transfer of part of personal allowance to spouse or civil partner (Chapter 2)

The optional election for a taxpayer to transfer a fixed amount of their personal allowance (PA) to their spouse/civil partner remains available for the tax year 2022/23. The conditions are unchanged from 2021/22 (so they are not repeated here).

3.4.1 The election

The election is to transfer a **fixed amount** of PA, regardless of actual unused PA, and is also referred to as the marriage allowance (MA). It is not possible to transfer more or less than the fixed amount.

Electing for the MA allows the transfer of £1,260 for the tax year 2022/23.

The figure of £1,260 is included in the tax rates and allowances provided to you in the examination, and is described there simply as the 'transferable amount'.

3.4.2 The effect of the election

The impact of this election on the two individuals' income tax computations is:

- the transferring spouse or civil partner's PA is reduced by the fixed amount (£1,260 in 2022/23)

- the recipient spouse's income tax liability is reduced by a maximum of £252 (being £1,260 MA × 20% BR income tax). If the recipient's income tax liability before applying this reduction is less than £252, no tax repayment is possible, but the amount by which the transferor's PA is reduced remains the full £1,260.

3.5 Changes to employment benefit rules (Chapter 5)

- Car and car fuel benefit (section 3.5.1)
- Van and van fuel benefit (section 3.5.2)
- Living accommodation and beneficial loans – no change in the official rate of interest (ORI) from 6 April 2021 (3.5.3)

3.5.1 Car and car fuel benefit

When calculating a car benefit, the relevant percentage still depends on the car's official CO_2 emissions.

In general the car benefits percentages for tax year 2022/23 as provided in the tax tables are 1% higher than they were for tax year 2021/22, for the same CO_2 emissions.

The percentage for electric-powered cars with zero CO_2 emissions is now 2%.

The percentages for electric-hybrid cars with emissions up to 50g/km depend upon its electric range which will be provided in the exam. Having identified this the relevant percentage can be found in the taxation tables, an extract of which can be found below.

Electric range	Relevant %
130 miles or more	2
70 to 129 miles	5
40 to 69 miles	8
30 to 39 miles	12
Less than 30 miles	14

- For a car with emissions of between 51 to 54g/km the relevant percentage is 15%.

- The base level of emissions is 55g/km. The relevant percentage to use here is 16%. For every complete 5g/km that this figure is exceeded an additional 1% is added to this figure.

- An additional 4% continues to be added to the percentage for cars with a diesel engine. Cars that meet the RDE2 standard are still exempt from the diesel supplement.

- The maximum percentage that can be applied to any car has remained at 37%.

The car benefit is reduced by any contributions made by the employee towards running costs other than fuel.

Once calculated the relevant percentage is still applied to the list price of the car to calculate the benefit. A deduction can be made from the list price for capital contributions of up to £5,000.

- The fuel benefit continues to apply and is calculated when any private fuel is supplied to an employee for which the employee does not pay in full.

- The fuel benefit is not reduced by any contributions made by the employee towards fuel, but does not apply if the employee reimburses the employer in full for private fuel.

- The fuel benefit base figure has increased to £25,300. This is given in your exam rates and allowances.

- The percentage to use in the calculation of fuel benefit remains the same as that used to calculate car benefit.

Illustration 3

Middleton plc provides the following vehicles for use by employees in 2022/23:

Angus is provided with a petrol driven car with CO_2 emissions of 109g/km from 6 August 2022. The list price of the car was £22,000 but Angus contributed £3,000 towards its purchase. Angus is provided with fuel for business and private purposes costing £780. He pays the company £200 towards the cost of fuel.

Balbir is provided with an electric-hybrid car with CO_2 emissions of 26g/km on 6 April 2022. The car has an electric range of 39 miles. The car cost the company £14,000 although its list price was £15,200. Balbir has all his fuel paid by the company. He does not contribute anything towards running costs of the car.

Ceris is provided with a car throughout the tax year 2022/23, which she uses 50% privately. The car has CO_2 emissions of 102g/km and Ceris is reimbursed for all her diesel fuel costs. The car has a list price of £85,000 and does not meet the RDE2 standard.

The assessable car and fuel benefits for these employees are calculated as follows:

	£
Angus	
Car benefit (£19,000 (W1) × 26% (W2) × 8/12 (W3))	3,293
Fuel benefit (£25,300 × 26% (W2) × 8/12 (W3))	4,385
Total assessable benefits	7,678
Balbir	
Car benefit (£15,200 × 12%)(W4)	1,824
Fuel benefit (£25,300 × 12%)(W4)	3,036
Total assessable benefits	4,860
Ceris	
Car benefit (£85,000 × 29%) (W5)	24,650
Fuel benefit (£25,300 × 29%) (W5)	7,337
Total assessable benefits	31,987

Workings

(W1) A deduction can be made from the list price for capital contributions of up to £5,000. This reduces the list price used in the calculation of the car benefit to £19,000 (£22,000 – £3,000).

(W2) Appropriate percentage

	%
Basic % for petrol car	16
Plus: (105 – 55) ÷ 5	10
	26

The CO_2 emissions figure of 109 is rounded down to 105.

(W3) Reduction for non-availability

The car was available for eight months of 2022/23 so the car benefit and the fuel benefit are apportioned by 8/12.

Alternatively the benefit can be calculated for the full year and reduced by 4/12.

(W4) The car is a hybrid with emissions not exceeding 50g/km therefore the relevant percentage depends on the electric range. This is between 30 to 39 miles meaning a percentage of 12%.

FINANCE ACT 2022 – THE IMPACT ON YOUR EXAM

> (W5) Appropriate percentage
>
> | | % |
> |---|---|
> | Basic % for petrol car | 16 |
> | Plus: (100 – 55) ÷ 5 | 9 |
> | Plus: supplement for diesel car not meeting RDE2 | 4 |
> | | 29 |
>
> The CO_2 emissions figure of 102 is rounded down to 100.

3.5.2 Van and fuel benefit

The flat rate benefit for private use of a van (other than a zero emissions van) in 2022/23 has increased to £3,600 per annum. This benefit is not charged if private use of the van is 'insignificant'.

If the van provided has zero CO_2 emissions then the benefit is exempt.

The annual scale charge for private use fuel provided for a company-owned van has increased to £688.

Both of the above rates are provided in the TX exam tax rates and allowances.

Electric vehicle charging facilities provided at or near the workplace do not count as a provision of fuel.

3.5.3 Living accommodation and beneficial loans – no change in official rate of interest

The official rate of interest (ORI) from 6 April 2022 is unchanged at 2%. This rate is provided in the exam rates and allowances. The following illustration reminds you how the ORI is used.

Illustration 4

Hussnan is provided with a house to live in by his employer throughout 2022/23. This accommodation is not job-related.

It cost his employer £160,000 in June 2018 and £40,000 was spent on improvements in December 2018. The house has an annual value of £4,000.

Hussnan is also provided with a loan at an annual interest rate of 1% by his employer, of £18,000, loaned to him 3 years ago. He has no other loans and has paid the employer interest only on a monthly basis.

Hussnan's taxable benefits for 2022/23 are:

	£
Accommodation	
Basic charge = annual value	4,000
Expensive accommodation	
(£160,000 + £40,000 – £75,000) × 2%	2,500
Loan	
£18,000 × (2% – 1%)	180
Total assessable benefits	6,680

KAPLAN PUBLISHING

TX-UK: TAXATION (FA2022)

4 BUSINESS INCOME TAX – No changes for tax year 2022/23

4.1 There are no changes made by Finance Act 2022 to the business tax rules or allowances in 2022/23 compared with the previous tax year. The same information as for the previous year's exams will be given in the exam tax rates and allowances (see Section C of this booklet).

5 PENSIONS (Chapter 6) – No changes for tax year 2022/23

5.1 There are no changes made by Finance Act 2022 to the pension tax rules or allowances in 2022/23 compared with the previous tax year. The same information as for the previous year's exams will be given in the exam tax rates and allowances (see Section C of this booklet).

6 NATIONAL INSURANCE CONTRIBUTIONS (NICs) (Chapter 12)

6.1 Key changes

The only changes to NICs rules within the TX syllabus for tax year 2022/23 are to the various NIC limits and rates which are all given in the exam rates and allowances (see tables in Section C).

6.2 Changes to rates and allowances

The new limits and rates are set out in the tax rates and allowances in Section C of this update booklet. The main changes are set out below.

The 1.25% increase in rates of NICs represents a 'health and social care levy', however it is included in the rate of NICs and does not need to be shown separately.

6.2.1 Class 1 employee's NICs

The earnings limit for class 1 employee's NICs has increased to £12,570. This represents the point at which employees start to pay NICs on their cash earnings.

The upper earnings limit for employee class 1 remains at £50,270.

The rates of class 1 employee NICs have increased to 13.25% on earnings between £12,570 and £50,270, and 3.25% on earnings above £50,270.

6.2.2 Class 1 employer's NICs

The earnings limit for class 1 employer's NICs has increased to £9,100. This represents the point at which employers start paying NICs on the employee's earnings.

There continues to be no upper earnings limit for employer's class 1 NICs.

The rate of class 1 employer NICs has increased to 15.05%.

6.2.3 Class 1A NICs

The rate of class 1A NICs has increased to 15.05%.

6.2.4 Class 2 NICs

The weekly rate for class 2 NICs has increased to £3.15 per week of trading.

The lower profits limit has increased to £12,570.

6.2.5 Class 4 NICs

For class 4 NICs the lower profits limit has increased to £12,570. This represents the point at which this class of NICs becomes payable.

The upper profits limit for class 4 NICs remains at £50,270. The rate of NICs payable reduces from this point.

The rates of class 4 NICs have increased to 10.25% on earnings between £12,570 and £50,270, and 3.25% on earnings above £50,270.

6.2.6 Employment allowance

The employment allowance (available to deduct from total employer's NICs for the tax year) has increased to £5,000 in 2022/23.

Illustration 5

Zaheer has a regularly paid salary of £52,220 throughout the tax year 2022/23. He also receives employment benefits valued at £6,400.

The NIC liabilities of Zaheer and his employer on his total pay in 2022/23 are as follows:

Employee's NICs	£
Employee's class 1	
Up to £12,570 × Nil	0
(£50,270 – £12,570) × 13.25%	4,995
(£52,220 – £50,270) × 3.25%	63
	5,058

Employer's NICs	£
Employer's class 1	
Up to £9,100 × Nil	0
(£52,220 – £9,100) × 15.05%	6,490
Class 1A	
Benefits (£6,400 × 15.05%)	963
	7,453

Illustration 6

Praveen is self-employed. His tax adjusted profits for the tax year 2022/23 are £60,000.

His total NIC liability for the tax year 2022/23 is as follows:

Class 4 NICs	£
Up to £12,570 × Nil	0
(£50,270 – £12,570) × 10.25%	3,864
(£60,000 – £50,270) × 3.25%	316
	4,180
Class 2 NICs	
(£3.15 × 52 weeks)	164

TX–UK: TAXATION (FA2022)

7 CAPITAL GAINS TAX (CGT) (Chapter 18 onwards)

7.1 Key changes

On disposal of a residential property the length of time to submit and pay the related tax has increased to 60 days.

All other CGT rates and allowances, all exemptions, reliefs and computational rules (within the TX syllabus) remain the same in 2022/23 and similar information is in the exam tax rates and allowances (see Section C).

8 INHERITANCE TAX (IHT) (Chapter 23) – No changes for tax year 2022/23

8.1 Key changes – none

No changes are made by FA2022 to any IHT rules.

The exam tax rates and allowances (see Section C) will only give one nil rate band for IHT- which is £325,000 – as this is the NRB applying for 14 tax years before 2022/23.

9 CORPORATION TAX (CT) (Chapter 14) – No changes for tax year 2022/23

9.1 Key changes

No changes are made by FA2022 to any corporation tax rules.

The rate of corporation tax for Financial Year 2022 is unchanged at 19%.

9.2 Enhanced capital allowances (Chapter 14)

The 130% super deduction and first year allowance at 50%, introduced in FA2021, continue to apply to companies in FA2022. Questions will not be set involving the disposal of an asset that qualified for the enhanced capital allowances, or with accounting periods spanning 31 March 2023 where there are any enhanced capital allowance purchases.

Illustration 7

Peacock Ltd has an accounting date of 31 March but changed this to 30 September in 2022 with a six-month accounting period ending 30 September 2022. At 1 April 2022 it had a main pool tax written down value (TWDV) of £Nil, and a special rate pool balance of £90,000.

In the six-month accounting period to 30 September 2022 the company spent £800,000 on new movable plant and machinery (no cars were included) and £1 million on new integral features incorporated into its factory building. There were no disposals in the period.

The maximum capital allowances for Peacock Ltd in the six months to 30 September 2022 are:

Period ended 30 September 2022	AIA £	FYA £	SRP £	Allowances £
TWDV b/f			90,000	
Additions: With super deduction				
Plant and machinery £800,000 × 130%		1,040,000		
Super deduction at 130%		(1,040,000)		1,040,000
Additions: With AIA		0		
Integral features	1,000,000			
AIA (Max £1,000,000 × 6/12)	(500,000)			500,000
Balance of special rate pool expenditure for FYA	500,000	500,000		
WDA (6% × 6/12)			(2,700)	2,700
			87,300	
Additions: With FYA				
Enhanced FYA at 50%		(250,000)		250,000
Transfer to SR pool			250,000	
TWDV c/f			337,300	
Total allowances				**1,792,700**

10 VALUE ADDED TAX (Chapters 24 and 25)

10.1 Key changes

From 1 April 2022 all VAT registered businesses will be required to use making tax digital (MTD), whether or not their turnover exceeds the registration threshold.

No other changes, within ACCA TX syllabus, are made by FA2022 to the VAT rules for tax year 2022/23, compared with those for the tax year 2021/22.

11 TAX ADMINISTRATION

11.1 Update of the key due dates in the TX syllabus

A summary of the key due dates for making elections and claims for the tax year 2022/23 is given in Appendix 4.

11.2 The interest rates to use in the examination (Chapters 13, 17 and 25)

The rate of interest on underpaid tax ('late payment interest') for use in the TX examination has increased to 3.25%.

The rate of interest on overpaid tax ('repayment interest') for use in the TX examination remains unchanged at 0.5%.

These figures are both given in your exam rates and allowances.

C TAX RATES AND ALLOWANCES

The tax rates and allowances below will be reproduced in the examination for TX for the June 2023 to March 2024 sittings.

SUPPLEMENTARY INSTRUCTIONS

1 **Calculations and workings need only be made to the nearest £.**

2 **All apportionments should be made to the nearest month.**

3 **All workings should be shown in section C.**

INCOME TAX

		Normal rates	Dividend rates
Basic rate	£1 – £37,700	20%	8.75%
Higher rate	£37,701 – £150,000	40%	33.75%
Additional rate	£150,001 and over	45%	39.35%
Savings income nil rate band	– Basic rate taxpayers		£1,000
	– Higher rate taxpayers		£500
Dividend nil rate band			£2,000

A starting rate of 0% applies to savings income where it falls within the first £5,000 of taxable income.

Personal allowance

Personal allowance	£12,570
Transferable amount	£1,260
Income limit	£100,000

Where adjusted net income is £125,140 or more, the personal allowance is reduced to zero.

Residence status

Days in UK	Previously resident	Not previously resident
Less than 16	Automatically not resident	Automatically not resident
16 to 45	Resident if 4 UK ties (or more)	Automatically not resident
46 to 90	Resident if 3 UK ties (or more)	Resident if 4 UK ties
91 to 120	Resident if 2 UK ties (or more)	Resident if 3 UK ties (or more)
121 to 182	Resident if 1 UK tie (or more)	Resident if 2 UK ties (or more)
183 or more	Automatically resident	Automatically resident

Child benefit income tax charge

Where income is between £50,000 and £60,000, the charge is 1% of the amount of child benefit received for every £100 of income over £50,000.

Car benefit percentage

The relevant base level of CO_2 emissions is 55 grams per kilometre.

The percentage rates applying to petrol cars (and diesel cars meeting the RDE2 standard) with CO_2 emissions up to this level are:

51 grams to 54 grams per kilometre	15%
55 grams per kilometre	16%

The percentage for electric cars with zero CO_2 emissions is 2%.

For hybrid-electric cars with CO_2 emissions between 1 and 50 grams per kilometre, the electric range of the car is relevant:

Electric range

130 miles or more	2%
70 to 129 miles	5%
40 to 69 miles	8%
30 to 39 miles	12%
Less than 30 miles	14%

Car fuel benefit

The base figure for calculating the car fuel benefit is £25,300.

Company van benefits

The company van benefit scale charge is £3,600, and the van fuel benefit is £688.

Vans producing zero emissions have a 0% benefit.

Individual Savings Accounts (ISAs)

The overall investment limit is £20,000.

Pension scheme limits

Annual allowance	£40,000
Minimum allowance	£4,000
Income limit	£240,000
Lifetime allowance	£1,073,100

The maximum contribution which can qualify for tax relief without any earnings is £3,600.

Approved mileage allowances: cars

Up to 10,000 miles	45p
Over 10,000 miles	25p

Capital allowances: rates of allowance

Plant and machinery
Main pool	18%
Special rate pool	6%

Cars
New cars with zero CO_2 emissions	100%
CO_2 emissions between 1 and 50 grams per kilometre	18%
CO_2 emissions over 50 grams per kilometre	6%

Annual investment allowance
Rate of allowance	100%
Expenditure limit	£1,000,000

Enhanced capital allowances for companies
Main pool super deduction	130%
Special rate pool first year allowance	50%

Structures and buildings allowance
Straight line allowance	3%

Cash basis accounting

Revenue limit	£150,000

Cap on income tax reliefs

Unless otherwise restricted, reliefs are capped at the higher of £50,000 or 25% of income.

CORPORATION TAX

Rate of tax	– Financial year 2022	19%
	– Financial year 2021	19%
	– Financial year 2020	19%
Profit threshold		£1,500,000

VALUE ADDED TAX (VAT)

Standard rate	20%
Registration limit	£85,000
Deregistration limit	£83,000

INHERITANCE TAX: tax rates

Nil rate band		£325,000
Residence nil rate band		£175,000
Rate of tax on excess — Lifetime rate		20%
— Death rate		40%

Inheritance tax: taper relief

Years before death	Percentage reduction
More than 3 but less than 4 years	20%
More than 4 but less than 5 years	40%
More than 5 but less than 6 years	60%
More than 6 but less than 7 years	80%

Capital gains tax: tax rates

	Normal rates	Residential property
Rate of tax — Lower rate	10%	18%
— Higher rate	20%	28%
Annual exempt amount		£12,300

Capital gains tax: business asset disposal relief and investors' relief

Lifetime limit — business asset disposal relief		£1,000,000
— investors' relief		£10,000,000
Rate of tax		10%

NATIONAL INSURANCE CONTRIBUTIONS

Class 1 Employee	£1 – £12,570 per year	Nil
	£12,571 – £50,270 per year	13.25%
	£50,271 and above per year	3.25%
Class 1 Employer	£1 – £9,100 per year	Nil
	£9,101 and above per year	15.05%
	Employment allowance	£5,000
Class 1A		15.05%
Class 2	£3.15 per week	
	Lower profits limit	£12,570
Class 4	£1 – £12,570 per year	Nil
	£12,571 – £50,270 per year	10.25%
	£50,271 and above per year	3.25%

RATES OF INTEREST (assumed)

Official rate of interest	2.00%
Rate of interest on underpaid tax	3.25%
Rate of interest on overpaid tax	0.50%

STANDARD PENALTIES FOR ERRORS

Taxpayer behaviour	Maximum penalty	Minimum penalty – unprompted disclosure	Minimum penalty – prompted disclosure
Deliberate and concealed	100%	30%	50%
Deliberate but not concealed	70%	20%	35%
Careless	30%	0%	15%

APPENDICES

		Page
1	Pro forma capital allowances computation – unincorporated businesses	29
2	Approach to capital allowance computational questions	31
3	Capital allowances illustrations	33
4	Time limits for elections and claims	36

FINANCE ACT 2022 – THE IMPACT ON YOUR EXAM

Appendix 1: Pro forma capital allowances computation – unincorporated businesses

	Notes		Main pool	Special rate pool	Short life asset	Private use asset (Note 2)	Allowances
		£	£	£	£	£	£
TWDV b/f			X	X	X		
Additions:							
Not qualifying for AIA or FYA:	(1)						
Second hand zero emission cars			X				
Cars (1g/km to 50g/km)			X				
Cars (over 50g/km)				X			
Car with private use						X	
Qualifying for AIA:							
Special rate pool expenditure	(3)	X					
AIA (Max £1,000,000 in total)		(X)					
Transfer balance to special rate pool				X			
Plant and machinery		X					
AIA (Max £1,000,000 in total)		(X)					
Transfer balance to main pool	(4)		X				
Disposals (lower of original cost or sale proceeds)			(X)	(X)	(X)	(X)	
			───	───	───	───	
			X	X	X	X	
BA/(BC)					X/(X)		X/(X)
Small pools WDA	(5)		(X)		0		
WDA at 18%							X
WDA at 6%				(X)			X
WDA at 6%/18% (depending on emissions)						(X) [× BU%]	X
Additions qualifying for FYAs:	(2)						
New zero emission cars		X					
FYA at 100%		(X)					X
		───	───	───	───	───	
TWDV c/f			X	X		X	
			───	───		───	
Total allowances							X
							───

KAPLAN PUBLISHING

Notes to the pro forma capital allowances computation

(1) Cars are pooled according to their CO_2 emissions into either the 'main' or 'special rate' pool.

New low emission cars receive 100% FYA.

(2) Cars with private use are de-pooled regardless of their CO_2 emissions and only the business proportion of allowances can be claimed.

However, the CO_2 emissions are important in determining the rate of WDA available.

(3) Allocate the AIA to the special rate pool expenditure in priority to plant and machinery assets as a WDA of only 6% is available on the special rate pool as opposed to 18% available on main pool items.

(4) Expenditure qualifying for AIA in the main pool which exceeds the level of AIA available is eligible for a WDA of 18%.

(5) Small pools WDA: can claim up to a maximum WDA of £1,000 but on the main pool and/or 'special rate pool' only.

(6) The taxpayer does not have to claim all or any of the AIA or WDA.

Differences for companies

This capital allowances pro forma in Appendix 1 is for unincorporated businesses.

The same pro forma can be used for companies, but must be adjusted for the following differences:

- Private use assets are not relevant.

- Companies have two additional (optional) capital allowances for new (unused) assets bought in the Financial Year 2022; these are not available to unincorporated businesses, so not shown in the pro forma.

- New main pool assets (other than cars) purchased between 1 April 2021 and 31 March 2023 are eligible for a 130% allowance (i.e. super deduction). This can be shown in the working column of the pro forma or as a separate deduction in the adjustment to profit computation.

- ACCA have stated that they will only test the super deduction for additions, but not the rules on later asset disposals, in the TX exams in June 2023 to March 2024.

- New special rate pool assets (other than cars) purchased between 1 April 2021 and 31 March 2023 are eligible for a 50% first year allowance. These additions can be dealt with in the standard pro forma in the workings column, with an FYA claim deducted and carried over to the allowances column. The cost balance after the FYA goes over to the SR pool as a final transfer in the capital allowances working, for carry forward to the next period.

- Exam questions will not test additions qualifying for the super deduction or the 50% FYA in a period straddling 31 March 2023.

Appendix 2

Approach to capital allowance computational questions

For plant and machinery capital allowances, adopt the following approach:

1. Read the information in the question and decide how many columns/pools you will require.

2. Draft the layout and insert the TWDV b/f (does not apply in a new trade).

3. For a company, at this point you must decide the extent of any claim for the enhanced capital allowances super deduction, if there is new main pool P&M which was acquired on or after 1 April 2021. If this is relevant, it is acceptable in ACCA TX to show that claim separately, completely outside the usual capital allowances pro forma, and to omit the relevant P&M additions from the other capital allowances working using the pools.

4. Insert 'additions not eligible for the AIA or FYAs' into the appropriate column taking particular care to allocate cars into the correct column according to CO_2 emissions, and also whether the car has an element of private use (not relevant for companies).

5. Insert additions eligible for AIA in the first column of your CAs computation and then deduct the relevant 100% AIA claims from the additions and enter the same AIA figures in the allowances column (right-side of the pro forma).

    - Remember to time apportion the AIA limit if the total CAs period is not 12 months long.
    - Always allocate the AIA to special rate pool additions in priority to main pool additions.

6. Any special rate pool additions in excess of the AIA must be added to the special rate pool column to increase the balance qualifying for 6% WDA in this period. Alternatively for companies the 50% FYA may be claimed on the excess expenditure rather than the 6% WDA.

    Any main pool expenditure in excess of the AIA should similarly be added to the main pool column, and if not £Nil will increase the balance qualifying for 18% WDA this period.

    The same approach is taken for non-AIA additions to any single-asset column.

7. Now deal with asset disposals in this period in the correct pool/column, by deducting the lower of the sale proceeds or the original asset cost.

8. Work out any balancing charge/balancing allowance for assets in individual pools. Remember to adjust for any private use if an unincorporated business (not relevant for companies).

9. Consider if the small pools WDA applies to the latest balance on the main pool and/or the 'special rate pool' and if so take it and enter the amount in the allowances column.

10. Calculate the WDA on each of the remaining pools which still has a positive cost balance, at the appropriate rate (either 18% or 6%), deduct it from the pool column and enter it in the allowances column.

    Remember to:
    - time apportion if the accounting period is not 12 months
    - adjust for any private use if an unincorporated business (not relevant for companies).

11 Insert additions this period eligible for FYAs in the additions column and deduct the appropriate FYA there and take it over to the allowances column. Transfer the balance of cost after FYA (even if it is £Nil) to the correct pool.

Remember that FYA is never time apportioned.

12 Calculate the TWDV to carry forward to the next accounting period and total up the right hand allowances column.

13 Deduct the total capital allowances from the tax adjusted trading profits.

Appendix 3

Capital allowance illustrations

Illustration 1

Lapse Ltd runs a manufacturing business and has always prepared its accounts to 30 November each year, but changed its accounting date in 2022.

During the eleven months ending 31 October 2022 Lapse Ltd incurred the following expenditure:

1 December 2021	Purchased a second-hand machine for £26,000. This is expected to last seven years and be worthless at the end of its life. The short life asset election is made.
1 January 2022	Spent £923,334 on a second-hand air-conditioning system for the factory building which is expected to last 20 years.
1 May 2022	Purchased a new fully-electric car for £27,000. This has zero emissions and is to be used by the production manager. Private use will be 25%.
1 July 2022	Spent £90,000 on a new lorry.
15 July 2022	Purchased a new car for £18,000 which will be used by the managing director. CO_2 emissions are 75 g/km and private use will be 20%.
5 August 2022	Purchased a new lift for the office building for £300,000.

In addition, on 1 July 2022 the company sold an old machine for £10,000 (original cost £15,000).

As at 1 December 2021 the tax written down values were as follows:

Main pool	£73,000
Special rate pool	£90,000

Lapse Ltd's capital allowances computation would be calculated as follows:

	AIA £	FYA £	Main Pool £	Special rate pool £	Short life Asset £	Allowances £
TWDV b/f			73,000	90,000		
Additions:						
No AIA/FYA						
Car – emissions exceeding 50 g/km				18,000		
Additions: With super deduction						
Lorry (£90,000 × 130%)		117,000				
Super deduction at 130%		(117,000)				117,000
Additions: With AIA			0			
Air conditioning (second-hand)	923,334					
AIA (Max £1,000,000 × 11/12) (Note)	(916,667)					916,667
Transfer balance to special rate pool				6,667		
Lift	300,000					
AIA (Max £1,000,000 × 11/12) (Note)	(0)					
Balance of special rate pool expenditure for FYA		300,000				
Machine	26,000					
AIA (Max £1,000,000 × 11/12) (Note)	(0)					0
Transfer balance to short life asset					26,000	
Disposal (lower of cost or sale proceeds)			(10,000)			
			63,000	114,667		
WDA (18% × 11/12)			(10,395)		(4,290)	14,685
WDA (6% × 11/12)				(6,307)		6,307
Additions: With FYA						
Enhanced FYA at 50% on balance of SRP expenditure		(150,000)				150,000
				150,000		
New Car – zero emissions	27,000					
FYA at 100%	(27,000)					27,000
			0			
TWDV c/f			52,605	258,360	21,710	
Total allowances						1,231,659

Notes: Super deduction is not available on the £26,000 machine and nor is SR pool FYA claim on the air conditioning, as they are second-hand purchases.

The lorry is eligible for 130% super deduction as it was purchased new after 1 April 2021. This should be given in preference to AIA since it gives greater relief.

The AIA is allocated to the additions in the 'special rate pool' (WDA 6%) in priority to the additions in the main pool (WDA 18%).

As the period is only 11 months, the AIA and WDA must be time apportioned. However, the FYA is never time apportioned.

There are no private use adjustments for companies; permitted private use of assets by company staff or directors is still business use by the company.

The new lift qualifies for 50% FYA but the balance is not eligible for WDA until the following accounting period.

Illustration 2

Jellena is in business as a sole trader and prepares accounts to 31 December each year.

During the year ending 31 December 2022 she incurred the following expenditure:

15 May 2022	Purchased new office furniture for £18,800.
2 June 2022	Purchased a new car with emissions of 90g/km for £26,667. Jellena will use the new car 20% of the time for private purposes.
10 June 2022	Installed a new water heating system in her business premises at a cost of £75,000 and a new lighting system at a cost of £8,000.

In addition on 1 July 2022 she sold office equipment for £2,200 (original cost £11,000).

As at 1 January 2022 the tax written down values were as follows:

- Main pool   £3,000
- Short life asset   £9,000

Jellena's capital allowances computation would be calculated as follows:

Jellena
Capital allowances computation for the year ending 31 December 2022

		Main pool	Special rate pool	Short life asset	Private use asset	B.U.%	Allowances
	£	£	£	£	£		£
TWDV b/f		3,000	–	9,000			
Additions:							
No AIA/FYA							
Car – emissions > 50 g/km					26,667		
Qualifying for AIA:							
Water heating and lighting systems		83,000					
AIA (Max £1,000,000) (Note)		(83,000)					83,000
			0				
Plant and machinery							
Furniture		18,800					
AIA (Max £1,000,000) (Note)		(18,800)					18,800
Disposal proceeds							
(lower of cost or sale proceeds)		(2,200)					
		800	0	9,000	26,667		
Small pool WDA		(800)					800
WDA at 18%				(1,620)			1,620
WDA at 6%					(1,600)	× 80%	1,280
TWDV c/f		0	0	7,380	25,067		
Total allowances							105,500

Note: The AIA is allocated to the additions in the 'special rate pool' (WDA 6%) in priority to the additions in the main pool (WDA 18%) but the order makes no difference here as the AIA is sufficient to cover all qualifying additions.

Appendix 4

Time limits for elections and claims

Income tax

Election/claim	Time limit	For 2022/23
Agree the amount of trading losses to carry forward	4 years from the end of the tax year in which the loss arose	5 April 2027
Current and prior year set-off of trading losses against total income	12 months from 31 January following the end of the tax year in which the loss arose	31 January 2025
Current and prior year set-off of trading losses against capital gains	12 months from 31 January following the end of the tax year in which the loss arose	31 January 2025
Three year carry back of trading losses in the opening years	12 months from 31 January following the end of the tax year in which the loss arose	31 January 2025
Three year carry back of terminal trading losses in the closing years	4 years from the end of the last tax year of trading	5 April 2027

Capital gains tax

Election/claim	Time limit	For 2022/23
Replacement of business asset relief for individuals (Rollover relief)	4 years from the end of the tax year in which the: – disposal is made, or – replacement asset is acquired whichever is later	5 April 2027 for 2022/23 sale or acquisition (if later event)
Holdover relief of gain on the gift of a business asset (Gift holdover relief)	4 years from the end of the tax year in which the disposal occurred	5 April 2027
Business asset disposal relief	12 months from 31 January following the end of the tax year in which the disposal occurred	31 January 2025
Determination of private residence	2 years from the acquisition of the second property	

Self-assessment – individuals

Election/claim	Time limit	For 2022/23
Pay days for income tax and class 4 NIC	1st instalment: 31 January in the tax year 2nd instalment: 31 July following the end of the tax year Balancing payment: 31 January following the end of the tax year	31 January 2023 31 July 2023 31 January 2024
Pay day for CGT on residential property disposals	Within 60 days of the disposal	
Pay day for other CGT and class 2 NIC	31 January following the end of the tax year	31 January 2024
Filing dates If notice to file issued by 31 October following end of tax year If notice to file issued after 31 October following end of tax year	Paper return: 31 October following end of tax year Electronic return: 31 January following end of tax year 3 months from the date of issue of the notice to file	31 October 2023 31 January 2024
Retention of records – Business records – Personal records	5 years from 31 January following the end of the tax year 12 months from 31 January following the end of the tax year	31 January 2029 31 January 2025
HMRC right of repair (i.e. to correct mistakes)	9 months from the date the return was filed	
Taxpayers right to amend a return	12 months from 31 January following the end of the tax year	31 January 2025
Taxpayers claim for overpayment relief	4 years from the end of the tax year	5 April 2027
HMRC can open a compliance check	12 months from the actual submission of the return	

TX–UK: TAXATION (FA2022)

Election/claim	Time limit	For 2022/23
HMRC can raise a discovery assessment		
– No careless or deliberate behaviour	4 years from the end of the tax year	5 April 2027
– Tax lost due to careless behaviour	6 years from the end of the tax year	5 April 2029
– Tax lost due to deliberate behaviour	20 years from the end of the tax year	5 April 2043
Taxpayers right of appeal against an assessment	30 days from the assessment – appeal in writing	

National Insurance Contributions

Election/claim	Time limit	For 2022/23
Class 1 employee's and employer's (or primary and secondary) – pay days	17 days after the end of each 'tax month' under PAYE system (14 days, if not paid electronically)	22nd of each month
Class 1 A NIC – pay day	22 July following end of tax year (19 July if not paid electronically)	22 July 2023
Class 2 NICs – pay day	Paid under self-assessment with balancing payment and CGT liability	31 January 2024
Class 4 NICs – pay days	Paid under self-assessment with income tax – within POAs and balancing payment	In POAs, and then 31 January 2024

Corporation tax

Election/claim	Time limit
Replacement of business asset relief for companies (Rollover relief)	4 years from the end of the accounting period: – in which the disposal occurred or – the replacement asset was acquired whichever is later
Set-off of brought forward losses against total profits (income and gains)	2 years from the end of the accounting period in which the loss is relieved
Current year set-off of trading losses against total profits (income and gains) and 12 month carry back of trading losses against total profits (income and gains)	2 years from the end of the accounting period in which the loss arose
Surrender of current period trading losses to other group companies (Group relief)	2 years after the claimant company's accounting period
Election for transfer of capital gain or loss to another company within the gains group	2 years from the end of the accounting period in which the disposal occurred by the company actually making the disposal

Self-assessment – companies

Election/claim	Time limit
Pay day for small and medium companies	9 months and one day after the end of the accounting period
Pay day for large companies	Instalments due on 14th day of: – Seventh – Tenth – Thirteenth, and – Sixteenth month **after the start** of the accounting period
Filing dates	Later of: – 12 months from the end of the accounting period – 3 months from the issue of a notice to deliver a corporation tax return
HMRC right of repair (i.e. to correct mistakes)	9 months from the date the return was filed
Company's right to amend a return	12 months from the filing date

TX–UK: TAXATION (FA2022)

Election/claim	Time limit
Company's claim for overpayment relief	4 years from the end of the accounting period
HMRC can open a compliance check	12 months from the actual submission of the return
Retention of records	6 years from the end of the accounting period

Value added tax

Election/claim	Time limit

Compulsory registration
– Historic test:
   Notify HMRC
 	
   Charge VAT
 	
– Future test:
   Notify HMRC
 	
   Charge VAT
	– 30 days from end of the month in which the cumulative turnover threshold was exceeded
	
	– First day of the second month after the taxable supplies exceeded the threshold
	
	– 30 days from the date it is anticipated that the threshold will be exceeded
	
	– The date it is anticipated that the threshold will be exceeded in the next 30 days (i.e. the beginning of the 30 day period)

Compulsory deregistration	30 days from cessation
Filing of VAT return and payment of VAT	One month and seven days after the end of the return period

Inheritance tax

Election/claim	Time limit	For 2022/23
Lifetime IHT on CLTs – pay day	Gift before 1 October in tax year – following 30 April Gift on/after 1 October in tax year – 6 months after the end of the month of the gift	30 April 2023
Death IHT on lifetime gifts within 7 years of death (CLTs and PETs)	6 months after the end of the month of death	
IHT on estate	6 months after the end of the month of death	
Transfer of unused nil rate band to spouse or civil partner	2 years from the date of the second death	